For Frank and Kitty.

Dimensional Illustrators, Inc.

Southampton, Pennsylvania

Batsford

PAPER
SCULPTURE
A STEP-BY-STEP GUIDE

Kathleen Ziegler
Nick Greco

Produced by **Dimensional Illustrators, Inc.**
Southampton, Pennsylvania USA

Published by **Rockport Publishers, Inc.**
146 Granite Street
Rockport, Massachusetts 01966 USA

Distributed to the book trade and art trade in the U.S. by:
North Light, an imprint of Writer's Digest Books
1507 Dana Avenue
Cincinnati, Ohio 45207
Telephone: 513.531.2222

Distributed to the book trade and art trade in Canada by:
McGraw-Hill Ryerson, Ltd.
300 Water Street
Whitby, Ontario L1N 9B6
Telephone: 800.565.5758
Fax: 800.463.5885

Other distribution by:
Rockport Publishers, Inc.
146 Granite Street
Rockport, Massachusetts 01966 USA
Telephone: 508.546.9590
Fax: 508.546.7141
Easy Link: 62945477

Address direct mail sales to:
Nick Greco
Dimensional Illustrators, Inc.
362 Second Street Pike/Suite 112
Southampton, PA 18966 USA
Telephone: 215.953.1415
Fax: 215.953.1697

Printed in Singapore
Library of Congress-in-Publication Data

PAPER SCULPTURE: A STEP-BY-STEP-GUIDE
Kathleen Ziegler, Nick Greco.

ISBN   0-7134-7567-6

Creative Director
Kathleen Ziegler
Dimensional Illustrators, Inc.

Executive Editor
Nick Greco
Dimensional Illustrators, Inc.

Copy Editor
Tom McClintock

Designer
Jennifer Dunn

Typography
Deborah Davis

Photography
Ken Yanoviak *Step-By-Step Photographs*
Kathleen Ziegler *Chapter Opening Photographs*
National Maritime Museum, Greenwich, England *Page 10*

Cover Illustration
Leo Monahan

Cover Photography
Lou Costy

Pantone® is a registered trademark of Pantone, Inc.

We wish to thank all the dedicated and talented professionals and friends for their assistance and support in bringing Paper Sculpture: A Step-By-Step Guide to fruition. Thanks to the exceptionally gifted paper sculptors from the United States, Canada and Denmark for their work and encouragement during the preparation of this text. Their patience and tireless efforts are to be applauded.

Special thanks to:

DEBORAH DAVIS for her dedicated work and typographic production.

JENNIFER DUNN for her elegant design and countless hours of hard work.

TOM MC CLINTOCK for reviewing, editing and refining the manuscript.

JONATHAN MILNE for his insight into the history of paper sculpture.

KEN YANOVIAK for his patience during the tedious hours photographing each step-by-step sequence.

GRAPHIC ARTISTS GUILD and Paul Basista for their assistance and counsel regarding artist's copyright laws.

NATIONAL MARITIME MUSEUM, Greenwich, England for their research assistance on paper sculpture.

STAN PATEY, BARBARA STATES and Staff of Rockport Publishers, Inc. for supporting our efforts on behalf of 3-Dimensional illustration.

Thank You All,
Kathleen Ziegler/Nick Greco
Dimensional Illustrators, Inc.

CONTENTS

INTRODUCTION

The communication revolution that was heralded by the advent of paper and paper processing also gave birth to a 3-Dimensional medium that continues to flourish today. There are accounts in China, as early as 105 AD, that detail the making of paper from scraps of fish netting, tree bark, rag and hemp. The production of paper increased markedly throughout the Middle Ages. During the early 16th century, Düren, Germany was recognized as a leading center for paper manufacturing. In the 18th century, Queen Anne of England is credited with constructing a paper ship cut with a penknife.

One notable precursor of paper sculpture in 18th century England was Augustine Walker. Two of his original maritime sculptures, circa 1760, are currently on exhibit at the National Maritime Museum, Greenwich, England. These magnificent paper caravels characterize his meticulous attention to detail. The Dutch paper sculptor A. Van Omeringh, a contemporary of Walker, is recognized for his conversion of Dutch sea paintings into paper sculptures. Unlike Walker's individual sea vessels, Van Omeringh captures the essence of the entire seascape. His work is preserved in the Art Gallery, Manchester, England and the National Maritime Museum, Greenwich, England.

During the industrial age, the production and perfection of commercial paper accelerated the availability and popularity of paper throughout the world. Although traditionally used as an artistic medium, window display artisans in London began using paper in their displays. With the advancements in photography, the windows were photographed and used as printed advertisements in magazines. As paper became more accessible, techniques evolved and it developed into a profitable illustrative medium. These early display sculptors were the harbingers of modern paper sculpture creatives. Paper sculptors Bruce Angrave and Arthur Sadler were pioneers of the contemporary paper sculpture industry. They were among the first illustrators in the advertising and editorial markets to use paper as an illustrative medium. The author of several books on paper sculpture, Sadler was influential in promoting paper sculpture as a commercial art form.

A. Van Omeringh, circa 1760. National Maritime Museum, Greenwich, England

Today, paper sculpture continues to spearhead the dimensional illustration industry. It is responsible for creating provocative solutions for the visual communications industry. The professional paper sculptors in this book, selected one project that represents their approach and method in creating paper sculptures. The step-by-step images provide insights into the creative process required to construct each project. Paper sculpture has become the focus of 3-D illustrators, modelmakers and creative directors who seek to explore the inherent appeal of paper as an illustrative medium.

The nine paper sculptors featured in this guidebook are all Gold or Silver award winners of the 3-Dimensional Illustration Awards Show. This unique, international juried competition is dedicated to showcasing the best in 3-D advertising and publishing worldwide. These prominent artists exemplify the best of the best from Canada, Denmark and the United States. The paper sculptors are divided into four distinct paper classifications: white papers, colored papers, painted papers and specialty papers. Their design methods and techniques are presented in easy-to-follow steps, intended to teach you the basics of paper sculpture assemblage. The universal appeal of paper sculpture, as a 3-D medium, is especially evident in the inspiring portfolios following each project.

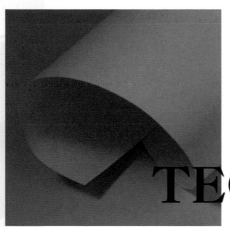

TECHNIQUES

Paper is a natural illustrative medium. Wood pulp, vegetable or cotton fibers arc beaten down, mixed with water and pressed into paper. This organic composition provides the tensile strength yet the flexibility needed for delicate manipulation. A flat piece of paper can be very deceiving. Those who recognize its versatility and limitations are gifted with a boundless palette from which to create.

Paper can be curled, rolled, folded or scored without tearing. A knowledge of flexibility, weight and texture, through hands-on application, will result in your ability to create paper sculpture images. With few cuts and gentle curves, paper is transformed from a flat surface into a 3-Dimensional network of light and shadow. Crush a piece of paper in your hand and gently flatten it out. Notice how the folds and creases enhance the overall dimension of the paper.

A variety of commercial and handmade papers are available in a wide range of textures and weights. Commercial papers such as Bristol, Strathmore and Canson are ideal for curling, scoring and folding. Bristol 2 and 3 ply papers are excellent selections for initial use. These papers are sold in Hot Press (smooth surface) or Cold Press (rough surface). Machine made paper only rolls smoothly in the direction of the grain. The grain is created during manufacturing. When paper is formed, the pulp fibers are aligned. This process allows the paper to be folded easily in one direction. Determining the grain of the paper is necessary before implementing any paper sculpture technique. Cut two sample pieces of paper and lightly fold the first piece of paper in one direction. Then, fold the second piece perpendicular to the fold of the first. The piece with the smoothest folded edge determines the direction of the grain.

Handmade papers offer the widest assortment of textures and weights. They are sold in commercial art stores and through handmade paper companies. These papers are made with acid-free substances which add longevity to the sculpture. Since handmade papers are not manufactured, their fibers are arranged in a random pattern. By eliminating the grain of the paper, it is easily manipulated or shaped in any direction desired. Handmade papers encompass thin Japanese rice papers as well as thicker watercolor and printmaking papers.

Curling, scoring and folding are the primary techniques used in paper sculpture. As you learn these fundamentals, you will understand and appreciate how light affects the paper surface. Curling is the technique that gives volume and dimension to the paper. It is achieved by rolling the paper to create a curved shape. This technique adds depth and illusion to the overall paper sculpture. The inner fibrous construction of paper allows for structural manipulation, provided it is rolled in the direction of the grain. Paper is curled by winding it around a cylindrical shape or by curving it along a straight edge. Wooden dowels or plastic triangles are the basic tools for curling paper. The specific elements of the image are cut out before curling. When shaping the paper, it should be rolled tighter than needed since it has a tendency to spring back slightly. Because paper is flexible, the same piece can be re-curled as often as necessary. This resiliency allows the paper sculptor freedom to reshape the paper while creating the sculpture.

Scoring employs the technique of cutting halfway through the paper thickness to provide a precise edge for folding the paper. It adds dimension by using angular flat planes which catch light and create shadows. A scored line is made by pulling a sharp #11 knife blade across the surface of the paper with a smooth gentle motion. To ensure a perfect fold, the scored line must be cut evenly. After cutting, the paper is folded away from the line, thus creating a smoother bend. Alternating score cuts on the front and back of the paper will create both concave and convex planes. Always use a new knife blade for cutting or scoring. The thickness of the paper will determine the exact pressure needed to create an efficient scored line. This technique involves both practice and patience to achieve satisfactory results.

The following pages will demonstrate the techniques of curling and scoring used to create basic paper sculptures. By experimenting with various papers and implementing the techniques of scoring and curling, you can create your own paper sculpture pieces. Mastery of these techniques is paramount in measuring your success as a paper sculptor. The image and style you produce is determined by the paper you choose coupled with your imagination.

1

Begin with two pieces of flat paper. Gently roll the first paper around the dowel, release and mark the direction of the grain. Roll the second piece in the opposite direction. The smoothest roll indicates the direction of the grain.

2

With one hand around the edge of the paper, gently roll the paper all the way around the dowel in the direction of the grain. Hold for a few seconds. The tighter the roll, the tighter the curl. A tighter curl can be achieved by rolling the paper with the fingers.

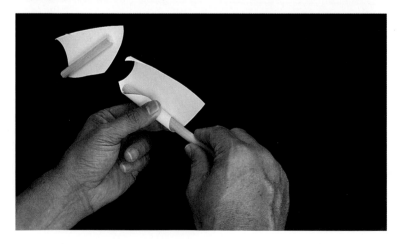

3

Release the paper from the dowel. The paper can now be shaped to achieve the correct curve by pushing it tighter or by opening it up.

CURLING

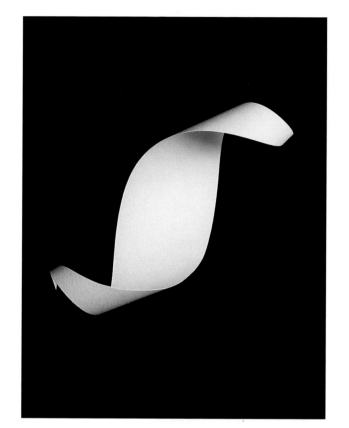

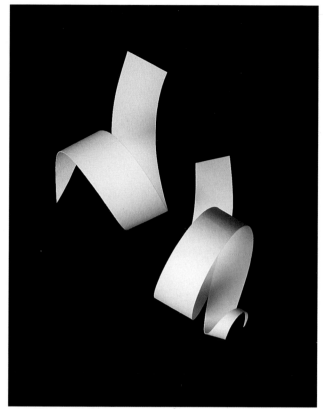

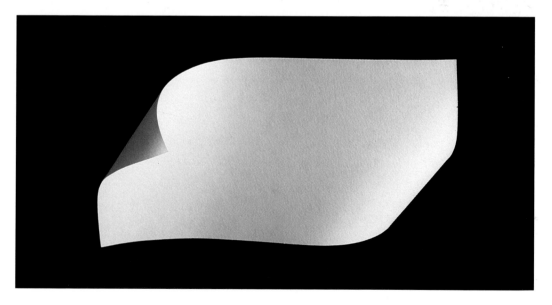

1

Draw with a pencil the exact shape to be cut. With a firm sharp blade cut out shape completely. Draw a line where the paper will be scored.

2

With both hands holding firmly on cut out image, gently cut halfway through the paper thickness on line drawn. Glide the knife with an even, smooth stroke across the surface.

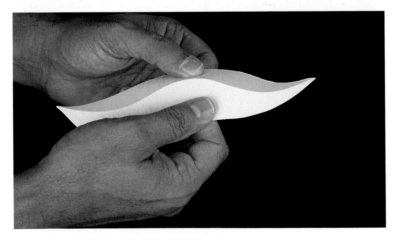

3

Lift shape with fingers underneath and thumbs on top. Push each side of the paper away with a gentle motion to bend the paper away from the scored line.

SCORING

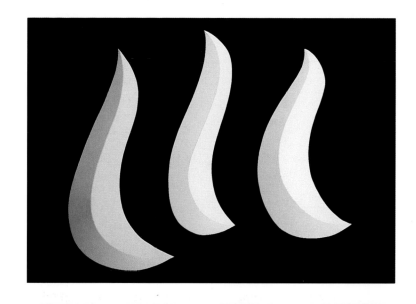

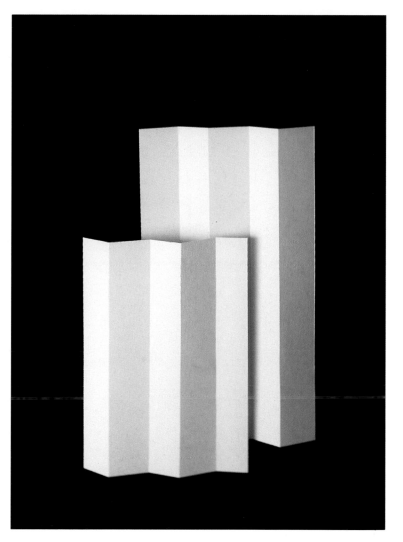

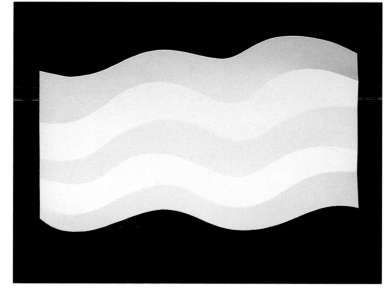

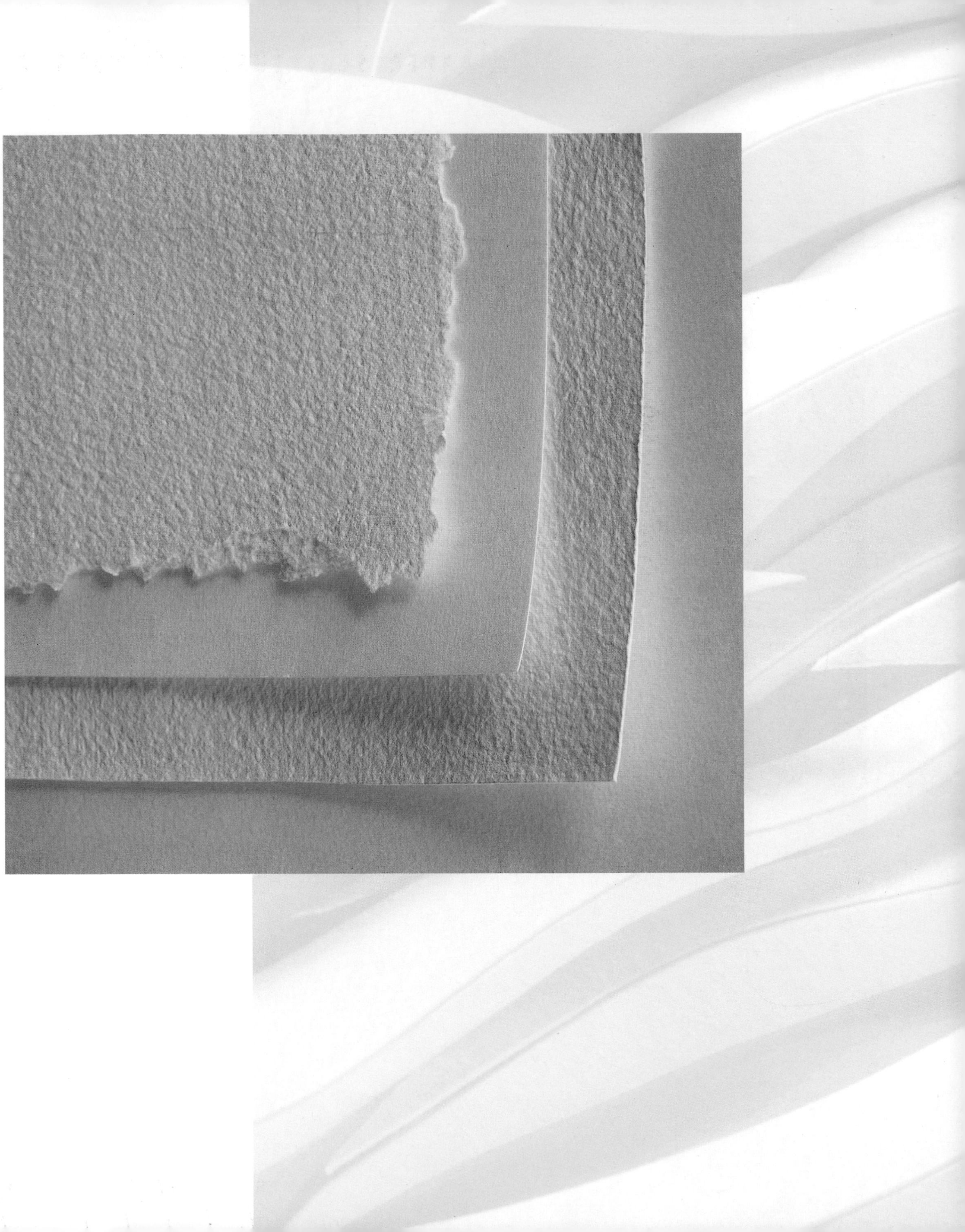

WHITE PAPERS

The pristine elegance of white paper sculpture is created by the subtle nuance of light and shadow. Herein lies the charismatic appeal, essence and grace of white paper sculpture. The signature works of Jonathan Milne and Johnna Bandle incorporate technical excellence and visual charm to produce a pure illustrative medium. Every compound curve transforms a basically flat surface into a compelling 3-Dimensional image.

The genre of white paper sculpture is artfully depicted in the works of Bandle and Milne. Bandle's methodical approach breathes life into the sculpture by pushing the paper to its absolute limit. Her work reveals a genuine vitality and charisma that is natural and radiant. Milne's purest style and attention to detail compels you to ignore the absence of color. His creation of compound curves using neither chisel nor lathe, are reminiscent of artists working in wood, stone or marble. Their work reflects a skilled blend of light and shadow that captures the essence and beauty of white paper sculpture.

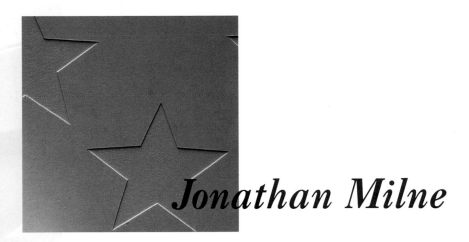

Jonathan Milne

Jonathan Milne now lives in British Columbia, but taught himself the art of paper sculpture while living in Australia. Early in his 18 year career, he realized that paper sculpture presented him the specialization he sought as a 3-Dimensional illustrator. He found it afforded him the spontaneity and flexibility to do advertising, editorial and gallery pieces. Using the paper as his palette, Jonathan's works are often of the classic "white-on-white" style, making him a true purist. He uses light and shadow to create visual effects, rather than applying paint or using colored papers. He has an intuitive command of the effects of light on the paper surface.

Jonathan is one of the artists responsible for the current awareness of paper sculpture in the communications industry. His efforts are helping to elevate 3-Dimensional illustration to equal status with its 2-Dimensional counterpart in the advertising and editorial industries. His ability to create intricate paper images helped stimulate the current use of such works for commercial purposes.

1

Several design styles for the Liberty Bell are sketched based on the original historic monument. White museum board of 1, 2 and 4 ply is chosen. This board cuts cleanly and holds its shape very well.

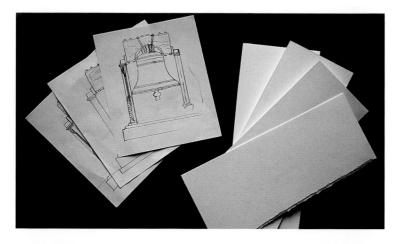

2

A tissue tracing of the bell is taped to the back of the 1 ply paper. The image is transferred by burnishing gently across the surface. Each structural element in the paper sculpture is completed and assembled later.

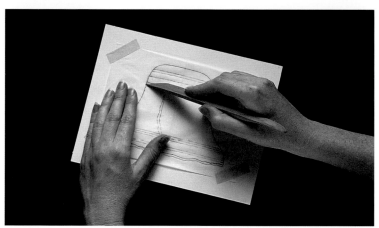

3

The blueprint image of the bell and all its parts are transferred to the paper. Each piece is cut out using a #11 blade. All pencil transfer lines are erased with a kneaded eraser.

4

The structural bands across the bell are created with scoring lines. A curved template is cut from 4 ply board. With a gliding motion the lines are scored into the back of the paper.

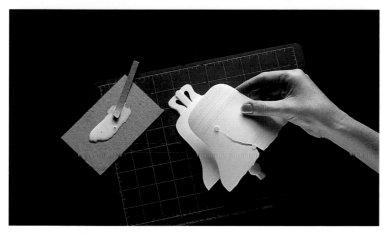

5

The edges of the bell are curled with the fingers around the perimeter surface rim. The dimensional character of the bell begins to take shape. All of the pieces for the bell are assembled and set aside.

6

A working drawing of the wooden bell hanger is created and transferred to the 1 ply paper. The background hanger structure is cut from 2 ply paper for support. A new blade is inserted then all the elements are cut out.

7

The support columns and filigree leaves are cut meticulously with 1 ply paper. Support rods, nuts and bolts are cut from 4 ply board. Blades are changed frequently when cutting 4 ply board to yield a solid cut edge.

8

The wooden detail of the hanger is made by scoring the back of the paper with a tool. This gliding motion creates the impression of wood grain. Periodically, the piece is held against a light source to get a reading of the surface texture.

9

An accurate outline of each letter used in the title is drawn to scale. They are transferred to 2 ply board using the burnishing method. Each letter is cut out with gentle slicing cuts.

10

Once all of the elements are completed, a 1/4" foamcore board is used as the background base. The stars and stripes are cut from 1 ply paper and applied to the surface.

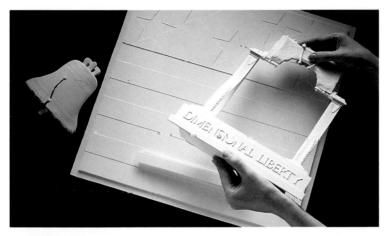

11

The wooden hanger is assembled and attached to the support columns. The decorative leaves are glued on top. All of the nuts, bolts and lettering are adhered into position.

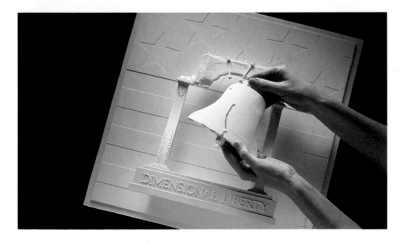

12

The bell is carefully joined to the entire structure. A clear plastic dowel is used to support the bell construction from the background.

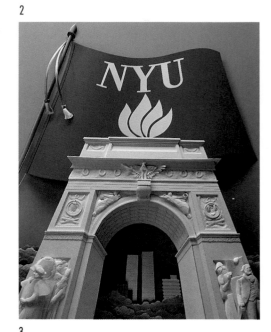

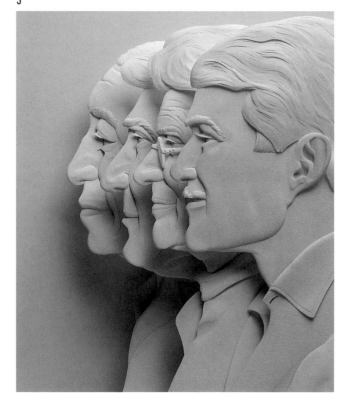

1
Gallery Artwork *Driving A Classic*
2
New York University *Fall Brochure Cover*
3
Glaxo Pharmaceuticals *Brochure Cover*

JONATHAN MILNE

4

5

6

4
Canada Post *Performing Arts Postage Stamp Series*
5
Radio Station CKLH 102.9 Hamilton, Ontario
Advertisement Campaign
6
Imperial Oil Canada *Commission For Shareholders*

7

8

9

7
Ontario Milk Marketing Board/Canada *School Poster Series*
8
Camden House Publishing/Canada Book Cover
9
Canadian Bank Note Company *Check Book Illustration*

10

12

10
Bank of Montreal *Booklet/Report Illustration*
11
Gallery Artwork *Sailing Vessel*
12
Reader's Digest Canada/USA *Image For Various Brochures*

13

14

15

13
Harrowsmith Magazine *Cover*
14
Shoppers Drug Mart *Calendar*
15
American Express Logo *Advertisement*

16

17

18

16
Spelga Yogurt *TV Commercial/Northern Ireland*
17
Scott Paper *Advertisement*
18
Sun Bank/Florida *Advertisement*

Johnna Bandle

Like many paper sculptors, Johnna Bandle felt "drawn to the textural aspect" of the medium. She has worked as a paper sculptor for 12 years, the last several as a freelance artist based in Lenexa, Kansas. Self-taught, she has a background in technical airbrushing methods and a wide variety of other related artistic styles. Although she often uses an airbrush in her work, Johnna's unique style features "white on white" paper sculptures. Experience has taught her the best papers to use and how to get the desired results.

Johnna has won various illustration awards, but claims that her work is often hard to categorize. Her ability to pre-visualize allows her to pay close attention to detail, something that is crucial when working with white paper forms. She is recognized for the uncompromising quality of her work and strives to add her singular touch to each sculpture. Her feeling is that the medium holds endless possibilities and new ideas, and times of experimentation are always on the horizon.

1

An initial sketch of the hibiscus flower within a heart is designed. An exact pattern is drawn for all the individual pieces needed to create the sculpture.

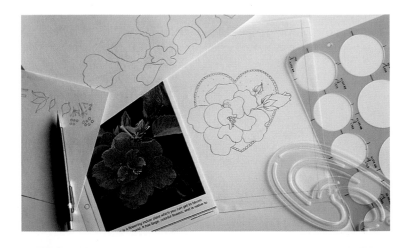

2

A selection of acid free white 1, 2 and 3 ply papers are chosen. Textured papers are preferred. The papers are cut to a workable size for the image and cutting mat.

3

The heart drawing is placed right side up on the carbon sheet. Using the french curve as a guide, the outline of the heart is traced onto the 1 ply white paper.

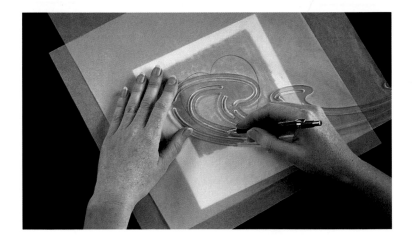

JOHNNA BANDLE

4

The decorative heart edge is transferred to the white paper from the carbon tracing. Carefully, using a #11 knife blade, the perimeter of the scalloped border is cut out.

5

After the inside heart is cut out, the edging is turned over. A piece of foamcore is placed under the paper and pins are used to create the detailed heart shaped ornamental border.

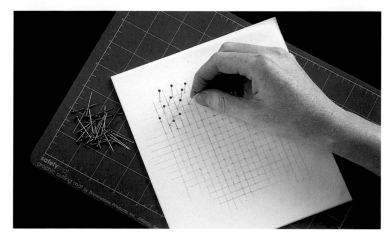

6

Background holes are created by placing a grid pattern over the mat board. Pins are inserted on the grid creating an overall even design of small precise dots.

7

Each individual petal for the hibiscus flower is accurately cut out from the 1 ply white paper using a #11 blade. The cutting mat helps to ensure a clean crisp edge for the smallest parts.

8

Textured veins of the petals are created by scoring the back of each with a wooden tool. Using a gentle gliding motion, creases are indented into the paper.

9

The curved petals are achieved by gently curling the edges and rolling between the fingers. As each petal is shaped, it is glued together from the center out.

10

Methyl cellulose acid free glue is used to attach all the elements together. The ornamental heart is positioned with foamcore spacers over the background grid.

11

The hibiscus flower petals are constructed in two layers. First the larger petals are positioned and glued. The smaller shapes are then attached in place. Foamcore is used to create space between the layers for added dimension.

12

Small parts are assembled and glued in the center of the blossom. Each tiny cluster is accurately attached and placed in the final selected position.

1

2

3

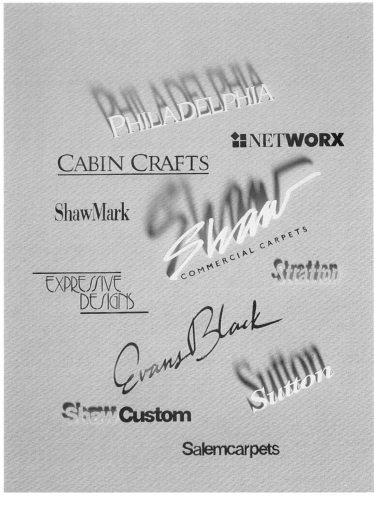

1
National Assn. of Insurance Companies *Poster and Brochure Cover*
2
Self Promotion *Louis Armstrong*
3
Shaw Industries *Logo/Annual Report Cover*

4

5

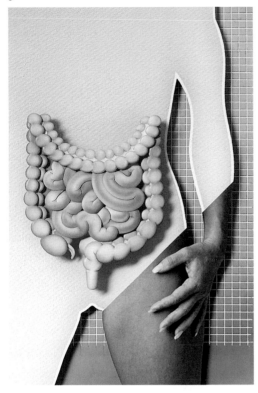

6

4
Manpower *Calendar Page*
5
Marion Merell Dow, Inc. *Cover Medical Pamphlet*
6
Macmillian-McGraw Hill *Children's Book Illustration*

7

8

9

7
Fesilor of America *Lens Promotion*
8
Sakura Bank Limited *Folder Cover*
9
Self Promotion *Art Nouveau Couple*

JOHNNA BANDLE

10

11

12

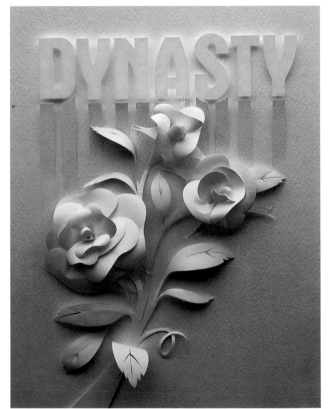

13

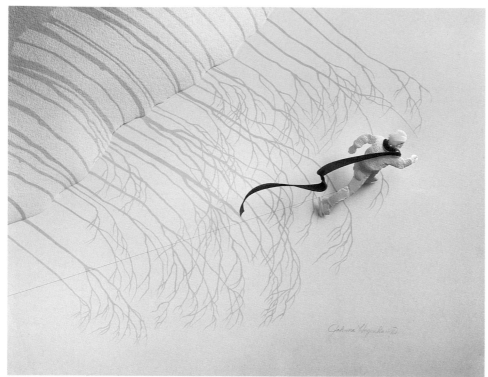

13
Manpower *Calendar Page*
14
Baxter, Burdick & Jackson *Albert Einstein Poster*
15
Commerce Bank *Yellow Page Insert*

14

15

16

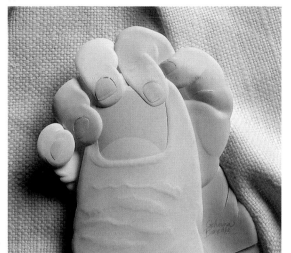

18

17

16
Personal Commission *Baptismal Present*
17
Hallmark Inc. *Wedding Shower Gift Wrap*
18
McDonald's *Christmas Promotion Wreath*

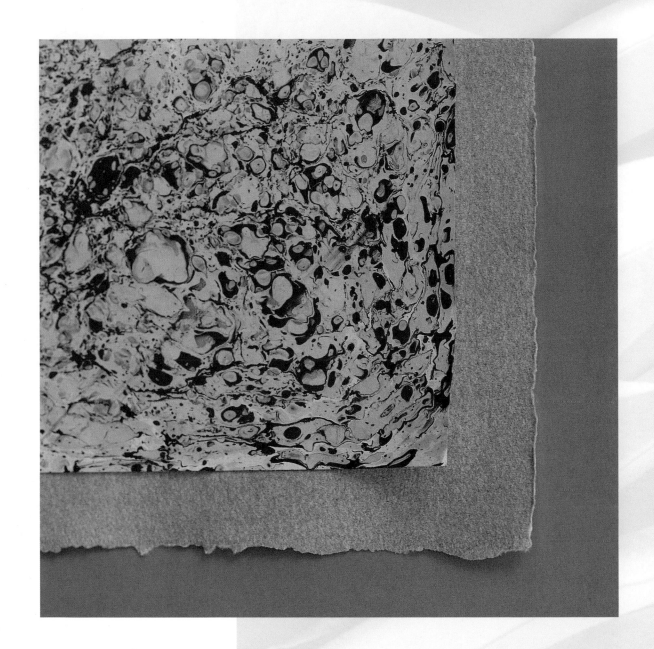

COLORED PAPERS

The graphic effect of colored paper, in the creation of paper sculpture, exemplifies the multifaceted components of this medium. The juxtaposition of colors amplifies the rich tonal variations of the paper and produces visually dynamic sculptures. Marbled paper affords the artist a complete range of patterns used to create the overall design. Colored paper provides the artist a complete range of shades used to illuminate the design.

The works of Hal Lōse and Søren Thaae are quite unique. Hal utilizes marbled papers to create his singular paper sculptures. He selects each pattern to insure the intrinsic color and tone of the design. His personal style is enhanced by the subtle variations of his handmade papers. Søren chooses standard colors for his paper sculptures. He carefully blends them to create a dynamic nuance of color harmony. His clean, crisp, paper sculptures evoke a sense of balance, stability and poise. Søren's work confirms his personal belief that paper sculpture reflects a human rather than a technological representation of his art. Both artists exemplify the philosophy that personal touch is a salient part of paper sculpture.

Hal Lōse

Hal Lōse began creating paper sculptures in 1969. He finds paper sculpture both a challenging and humorous form of illustration. Hal studied art at the Pennsylvania Academy of Fine Art, the University of the Arts and the Art Institute of Pittsburgh. Currently, he has his own design studio in Philadelphia. His style is enhanced by the diversity of papers he uses including his own marbled papers, handmade papers, Canson Mi Teintes and Canson Ingress. Hal prefers working with his own handmade marbled papers. The random design patterns add a special dimension to his paper sculptures.

Through the marbling technique, Hal incorporates a personal color style, texture and feeling into his sculptures. During his professional career, he has produced an extensive collection of marbled papers. He enjoys the challenge of working with a medium that affords him the freedom of artistic discovery. This independence enables him to apply his talents to a wide range of styles and provides the opportunity to face new artistic and technical problems.

1

Rough sketches are drawn to indicate the pieces that will create the elements for the sun. Thumbnail ideas are jotted down showing construction details. A full size drawing is used as a pattern for the image.

2

Marbling for the flame patterns is created on large sheets of colored papers. Colors are floated on the top of specially treated water and a design is developed using various rakes and combs. The colored paper is then placed on the surface of the water and the design is transferred.

3

Variations on the flame patterns are marbled on different colored papers with different paint color combinations. Papers are selected that retain the strongest graphic statement for the finished sculpture.

HAL LŌSE

4

The flame shape and other parts of the paper sculpture are cut with an Exacto knife blade #11. The ends of the flame are then bent and twisted with a bone folder to help catch the light and shadows.

5

Various flame patterns are cut from the selection of marbled papers. Several photocopies of the face are made. They are cut out and slightly curved three dimensionally. This will indicate how the face will work on the flame patterns.

6

The development of the face is an ongoing process. Several faces are drawn, photocopied and temporarily assembled. The decision to marble the lips, eyebrows, iris and eyelids is made at this time. The circular face is constructed from a sheet of cream colored Mi Teintes paper.

7

Once the marbled papers are selected, a pencil drawing of the face is taped to the back. The two sheets are viewed on a light box to re-position the pencil drawing with the area of marbling that is chosen. Then, the parts of the face are traced onto the back of the marbled paper.

8

The shapes are cut out using the traced pencil line as a guide. Smooth flowing cuts are essential. If the cut veers off the pencil line, it is corrected or a new one is cut.

9

The pieces are then shaped with pressure from a bone folder, triangle or finger. In extreme cases, a humidifier is used to relax the fibers of the paper, which allows for complex curves. Once dry, they retain their position.

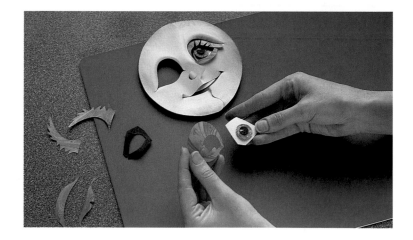

10

A fine spray of gold is applied to the edge of the circle to add dimension and sparkle when photographed. The face is assembled by attaching the features with One Coat rubber cement and masking tape. These adhesives allow for relocation and final adjustments during photography.

11

Layers of foamcore are inserted to create shadows. The completed sun has 3 layers of paper with 4 layers of foamcore in between. This raises the face approximately 4" above the background.

12

The pieces are glued into position with rubber cement. Different lighting techniques are achieved to create interesting shadows that add dimension. Art direction for the photography is provided by the artist.

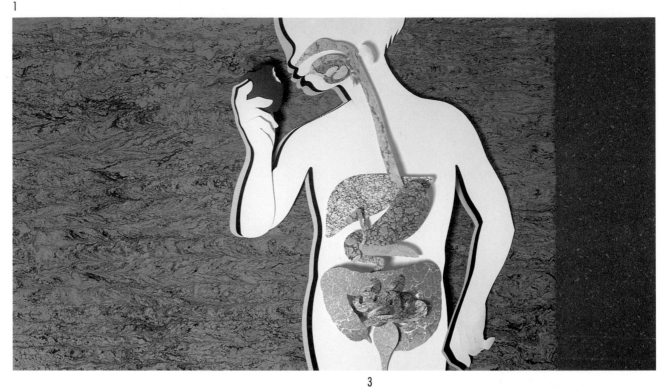

1

2

3

1
Whittle Communications *Educational Poster*
2
Macmillian/Hampton Brown *Children's Book*
3
Prudential Dental HMO *Spread Advertisement*

4

6

5

4
ARA Food Service *School Poster*
5
Dow Jones Magazine *Cover*
6
Witchwood Ice Cream *Poster*

7

8

7
Drug Topics *Cover*
8
Gallery Artwork *Bat Woman*

9

11

10

9
Gallery Artwork *Sun Image*
10
Gallery Artwork *Sun Image*
11
Gallery Artwork *Moon Image*

12

13

14

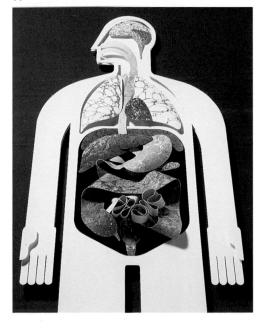

12
TCG *Calendar*
13
American Showcase *Advertisement*
14
Smith Kline Beecham International *Ad and Brochure*

15

16

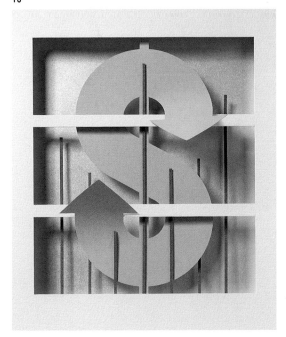

17

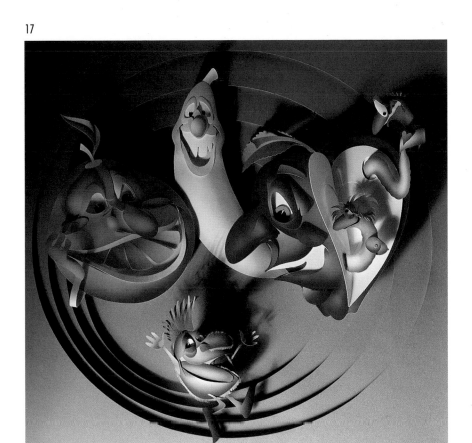

15
Macmillian Publishing *Math Book Cover*
16
Scott Paper *Cover Sales Manual*
17
American Showcase *Advertisement*

Søren Thaae

Since paper sculpting is an age-old tradition in his native Denmark, Søren Thaae believes he comes by his talent rather naturally. His exposure to paper sculpture came from making traditional figures for Easter and Christmas festivals in Copenhagen. Although he works mostly in the advertising industry, Søren has written several books on the techniques of Danish paper cutting. His background includes commercial art and freelance design. He also worked as a designer for Lego Toys in Denmark.

Søren uses brilliant, bold colors to enhance his traditional paper sculptures. His crisp, graphic style reflects the influence of the Scandinavian manner of working with paper. His figures and images are highly stylized, but reflect the individual human touch of the artist. Søren feels that paper sculpture affords him the opportunity to add the personal elements which distinguish his work from conventional 2-Dimensional illustration. Intrigued by the "realness" of working with paper, he believes in a representational rendering of his subjects. He savors the idea that paper sculpture does not normally have a "high-tech" gloss to it. Paper sculpture should give you the feeling "it is made by hand and not through technology."

1

After many draft sketches are drawn, a final color design is prepared. Ten different colors of Canson, PANTONE® and Canford papers are chosen to match colors of the wreath.

2

Individual patterns of each element are drawn except the leaves and flowers. Several photocopies of the images are reproduced then stapled to the specific colored papers needed.

3

The photocopy pattern is placed over the colored paper and the animals are cut out. A cutting board is used to ensure a clean precise cut.

SØREN THAAE

4

The flower components are cut from various shades of green paper. A square paper is folded in half. Without drawing a pattern, a scissor is used to cut two flowers at one time.

5

With this freehand scissor technique, the flowers are more organic in contour and shape. The center of the flowers are attached with small pieces of 1/8" foamcore.

6

All the green paper leaves are cut freehand with the knife. To achieve the precise points on the leaves, the knife blade must be changed often.

7

The rabbit is cut from grey Canson paper. Very small circles are stamped out of adhesive black paper with a variable hole punch for the eyes.

8

After the chicks and hen are cut, the beaks are formed from folded paper. All the elements are then carefully adhered with foam tape and attached with tweezers.

9

The wreath base is fabricated from durable 2 ply Bristol paper. The circular ring is first drawn with a compass, then cut out with scissors.

10

The elements are assembled in layers. The large hen piece is placed in position and the flower parts are arranged under and on top of the base.

11

The components are attached with foamcore tape. Once the layers are adhered, the remaining pieces are integrated into the wreath with tweezers.

12

The leaf blades are curled with the fingers while in place. Final adjustments are made by slightly shifting the pieces until a desirable composition is achieved.

1
Shell Denmark *Advent Calendar*
2
EL NYT Periodical *Cover*
3
Baltica Insurance Company *Leaflet/Wage Security*

4

5

6

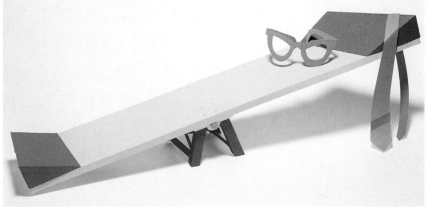

4
Baltica Insurance Company *Advertisement/Travel Insurance*
5
Baltica Insurance Company *Advertisement/Household Insurance*
6
Baltica Insurance Company *Educational Poster*

7

7
The Image Bank/USA *Industry Advertisement*
8
Duracell Batteries *Poster*
9
Baltica Insurance Company *Leaflet*

9

8

10

12

10
Hetland Sparbank *Poster*
11
Unicef *Greeting Card*
12
Baltica Insurance Company *Leaflet/Annuity*

13

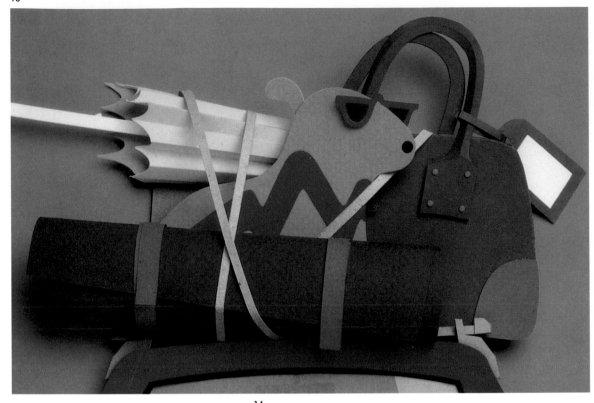

14

13
Baltica Insurance Company *Billboard*
14
Baltica Insurance Company *Advertisement Board*

SØREN THAAE

15

16

15
Baltica Insurance Company *Advertisement*
16
Klip Til Paaske *Book Cover*

PAINTED PAPERS

The union of paint and paper present the viewer with a remarkable textural perspective. By applying paint to the paper surface, the artist adds depth, shadow and texture to the paper sculpture. Color gives volume and dimension to the object, and allows the artist to introduce tonal variations, creating a *trompe-l'oeil* effect. There are diverse methods used to add color to a paper sculpture. Each technique brings a subtle nuance of shade, color and weight. In this chapter, the artists use sponging, spattering and airbrushing methods to obtain provocative textural variations.

The works of Leo Monahan, Sally Vitsky and Gus Alavezos demonstrate three distinct methods of painted paper techniques. Monahan's sponging technique adds a spontaneous overall texture to his paper sculptures. His rich colors and tonal changes bring warmth and charisma to the sculpture. Sally Vitsky uses a toothbrush to apply paint to the surface of the paper. Her spattering technique adds color and weight to the sculpture in a natural freestyle manner. Gus Alavezos uses an airbrush to attain the vibrant colors and gradual tonal qualities so characteristic of his paper sculpture style. All three approaches show the diversity of textural motifs created by the fusion of paint and paper.

Leo Monahan

With more than 30 years of experience, Leo Monahan has developed his own paper sculpture style, yet has remained true to the early artistic influences in his life. As a child in South Dakota, he became familiar with American Indian motifs that are still evident in his work today. Like most paper sculptors, he is self-taught, relying on his own spontaneity and intuition to guide the knife along the paper. Leo specializes in drawing with the knife, rather than first with a pencil. He finds that sculpting in this manner adds integrity to the creation of his work. His techniques for adding color to his work include sponging, airbrushing and dry pigment application.

His philosophy of paper sculpting is true to its form. He is intrigued by the manipulation of light upon plain and colored surfaces. Monahan creates and consistently refines his work until the point of completion. His dedication to the art of paper sculpture has earned him numerous professional accolades including a life achievement award from the Society of Illustrators in Los Angeles.

1

The sketches are drawn to scale with a pointed marker indicating the elements needed for the paper sculpture. The large sketch of the swan is used for the basic structure and attitude.

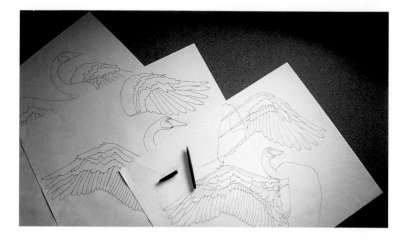

2

Papers selected are 500 series Strathmore 2 and 3 ply kid finish drawing Bristol. Handmade paper is preferred in the construction of the water and background. Acid free museum board is chosen for the overall background support.

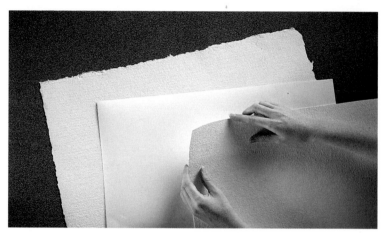

3

Acrylic cel-vinyl paint is mixed to create original colors for the specific project. Sponging is imprinted on the surface of the paper creating an overall organic applied texture.

LEO MONAHAN

4

A mono-printing technique is utilized for the swan.
A sponged texture is applied to one surface, then
blotted onto another surface. The swan is sponged
first, then mono-printed with white paint.

5

The sketch is transferred on a light box face down so
that the pencil lines are on the back surface of the
painted paper. Each shape is drawn separately and
is only a guide for cutting.

6

Cutting is done by drawing with the #11 knife blade.
The blade is changed often and never sharpened.
Pieces of the swan wing are cut out. The line followed
by the knife is never the same as the drawn line.

7

Each piece of the swan is cut out in sections. The pencil line is only used as a guide. Many of the shapes are cut freehand as needed and are not drawn exactly from the pattern.

8

Each piece is curled by wrapping the cut element around a dowel with the thumb and forefinger. Other curled shapes are achieved by pulling across a plastic triangle.

9

All of the curled elements for the swan are adhered with acid free glue. Each section is assembled in layers beginning at the bottom. The wings are constructed in the same manner.

10

The paper for the grass is painted with cel-vinyl paints. Colors for the palette are designed by mixing basic colors. Only a sponging technique is used for the overall surface composition.

11

The grass is cut from the sponged green paper. Each piece is sliced freehand. Pencil lines are not used as a guide. This technique allows for a more organic approach to the pieces.

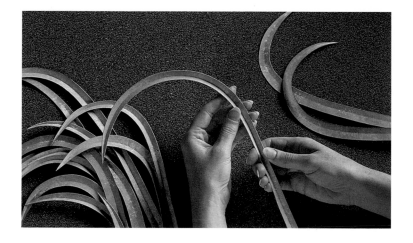

12

The grass pieces are scored freehand with a #11 blade. Many more elements are constructed then are needed. After each piece is cut out, it is carefully bent with the fingers along the scoring line.

13

Individual colors are mixed from basic colors to achieve a natural effect. Handmade papers are then sponged with the cel-vinyl paints for the overall background and water.

14

The best hand-sponged papers are selected for the fabrication of the paper sculpture construction. Since the design process is on going, more are created than used.

15

The background museum board is mounted to a 1' x 1' frame that has a piece of double weight board stapled to it. The background sky is attached using deep foamcore spacers. The paper should appear to be natural and not precisely flat.

LEO MONAHAN

16

Once the swan is assembled, it is mounted over the background using a sturdy wood spacer. Strong acid free glue is used to hold the complete swan construction in place.

17

The hand-sponged paper is mounted in two layers over the swan and in the background framing piece. The paper for the water, is ripped as needed to create the effects.

18

Curved slices are made in the water to insert the grass. This is done in place and not planned in advance. The grass is tucked around the swan to achieve overlaps and deep space. It is a growing piece that is constructed as it is created.

1
Technocell GMBH/Germany *Show Poster*
2
Hammermill Paper *Ad Insert and Poster*
3
Technocell GMBH/Germany *Calendar*

1

2

3

LEO MONAHAN

4

5

6

4
CBS Radio *USC Football Billboard*
5
Hammermill Paper *Ad-Insert and Poster*
6
Gallery Artwork *Indian Shield*

7

Gallery Artwork *Indian Costume*

8

Batey-Poindexter *Varig Airlines Billboard*

9

Eddie Bauer Corporation *Catalogue Cover*

7

8

9

10

11

12

10
Judy Instructo *Catalogue Cover*
11
Hollywood Bowl *Israeli State Orchestra*
12
Microsoft *Brochure Cover*

13

14

15

13
Saatchi & Saatchi *Advertising Poster*
14
Gallery Artwork *Indian Shield*
15
Gallery Artwork *50 Trees*

16

18

17

16
Doyle Research/Chicago *Office Decor*
17
Canadian Bank *ATM Advertisement*
18
Technocell GMBH/Germany *Calendar*

Gus Alavezos

Gus Alavezos is a self-taught paper sculptor with 14 years experience. He enjoys working with a variety of textures and colors. A graduate of the Academy of Art College in San Francisco, he currently lives and works in Monument, Colorado. The challenge of paper sculpture affords him the opportunity to experiment with a wide range of available papers to achieve his unique paper sculpture style. By using designer gouaches, watercolors and acrylics, along with an airbrush, he produces vibrant color combinations that are characteristic of his work. He uses colored, construction and charcoal papers, but prefers Strathmore paper because of its smooth, regular surface.

Unlike traditional paper sculptors, Gus uses a knife in conjunction with rulers, French curves and templates for mechanical cuts. Gus's paper illustrations are geared towards manipulating both color and paper to create brilliant and provocative dimensional pieces. He believes he can achieve more effective color combinations with paper sculpture, rather than mixing paint on a flat 2-Dimensional illustration. His playful illustrations demonstrate his ability to express humor through art.

1

After a preliminary cartoon style sketch of the bobcat is drawn, a precise image is made indicating the exact shape of the model to be constructed. The sketch acts as a blueprint for the paper sculpture pieces.

2

Several photocopies are made of the pattern. Then, the image is mounted with spray adhesive into position on Strathmore paper. Each individual piece will be cut from the paper patterns.

3

A sharp knife with a #11 blade is used to cut out the patterns through the two layers of paper. All the elements are cut out entirely before curling, scoring or painting.

GUS ALAVEZOS

4

A wooden dowel is used to curve the intricate sections of the bobcat's face. By applying pressure with both thumbs, the pieces are gently rolled around the perimeter of the dowel. This effect creates a curl in the paper.

5

After each section is cut, the blueprint pattern is peeled away and the model begins to take shape. Rubber cement thinner is used to remove the spray adhesive from the back of the paper.

6

Each section for the assembly of the rock is scored with the knife. The scored lines are cut halfway through the thickness of the paper. With the thumbs and forefingers, the pieces are carefully bent along the scored line.

7

The four sections of the rock are painted then assembled.
First, blue paint is airbrushed on the overall surface of the
paper pieces. Then, white Designers Gouache is applied
with a toothbrush to create a textural effect.

8

Similar values of orange and brown are mixed for the
bobcat. As the colors are combined, several tests are
applied to the paper before the final color is achieved.
The mixed pigment is prepared for the airbrush by
thinning with water.

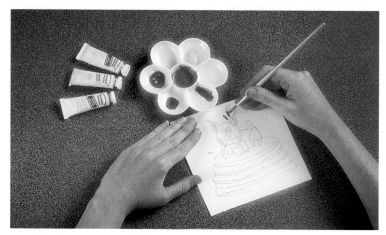

9

Using a Paasch AB airbrush, the prepared color is put in
the metal paint pot. After several tests are made, the parts
are sprayed with a light gradation of orange and brown
gouache. The details of the whiskers, ears and tail are
enhanced with brown areas of paint.

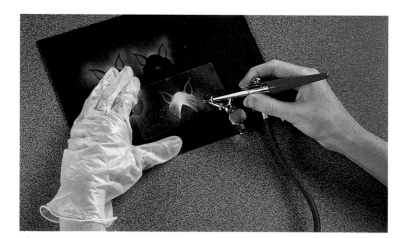

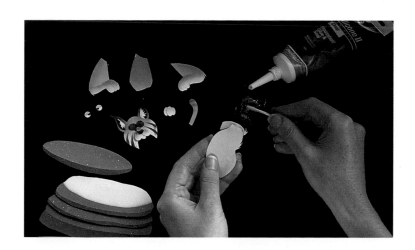

10

After the paint has dried, all the pieces are positioned and attached with silicone glue. This slow-drying, transparent adhesive, allows for any final re-positioning of the components for the model.

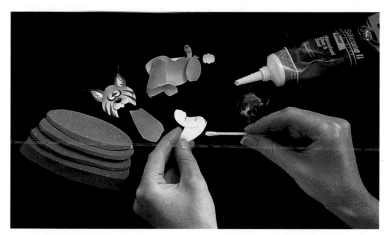

11

The curled and painted parts for the bobcat's body are carefully glued together. Small foamcore spacers are inserted and glued in between the pieces for depth and dimension.

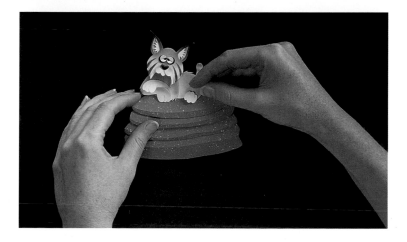

12

The small painted components for the face and head are connected and assembled. Final adjustments are made by additional curling with the fingers around the perimeter of the model.

1

2

3

1
Milton Bradley *Puzzle Game*
2
Self Promotion *White Tiger*
3
Self Promotion *Who's The New Toon In Town?*

GUS ALAVEZOS

4

6

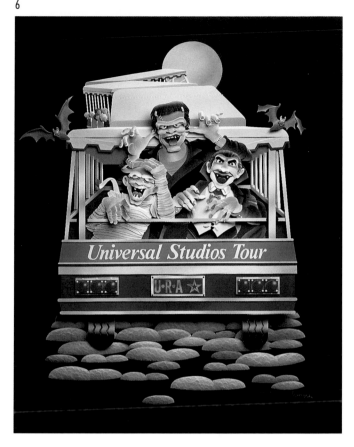

4
Milton Bradley *Puzzle Game*
5
RV Campers and Trailers *Illustration*
6
Self Promotion *Universal Studios*

7

7
Bank of Denver *Brochure*
8
Yankee Magazine *Cover Illustration*
9
Crown Zellerbach *Brochure*

8

9

10

11

12

10
Atlantic Monthly *Brochure*
11
IBM *Brochure*
12
Peninsula Magazine *Cover Illustration*

13

15

14

13
Hilton Hotel *Brochure*
14
Milton Bradley *Puzzle Game*
15
Current Inc. *Anniversary Card*

GUS ALAVEZOS

16

17

18

16
Kraft Cookbook *Illustration*
17
Kraft Cookbook *Illustration*
18
AT&T *Brochure*

Sally Vitsky

Richmond, Virginia based Sally Vitsky has worked as a paper sculptor for 15 years, but admits to an interest in paper creations since childhood. Self-taught, she also credits other paper sculptors with adding to her 3-Dimensional education. She is conscious of the quality and texture of the papers she chooses for each project. Sally usually strives for a stylistic interpretation of an image, which gives her a more graphic approach to the paper medium. She often uses textural techniques to add color to the paper surfaces. Paint may be splattered with a toothbrush, daubed with a soft cloth, airbrushed or sponged onto the paper. These techniques add depth and shadow to her creations. Sally prefers Bristol board, PANTONE® and Canson papers for her sculptures. She will use whatever she feels works for a particular piece and has created sculptures from sandpaper, newspaper and paper towels.

She enjoys the tactile aspect of sculptural work, and finds "the finished product, when printed commercially, has an almost surreal effect." She believes her sculptures give new life to charts and graphs and add a dimension that makes the viewer want to reach out and touch the illustration.

1

Several sketches are drawn on grid paper until the final idea is resolved. A paper sculpture window frame will be constructed utilizing several leaves and an intricately designed column in the foreground. A view of the beach with water will be in the background.

2

Two shades of blue PANTONE® uncoated paper are selected for the water. Tan and orange uncoated PANTONE® papers will be used for the beach scene and 2 ply Bristol paper is chosen for the column.

3

A photocopy of each individual leaf is made. They are then attached with masking tape to the front surface of the green uncoated PANTONE® paper. The leaves are cut through the pattern with a #11 knife blade.

SALLY VITSKY

4

Green pastel is used to darken the edges of the leaves. The chalk is crushed and applied with a finger in a circular motion around the perimeter edges of the leaves. The back of the leaves are gently scored with the knife.

5

Since the green PANTONE® paper has ink only on the top surface, once cut, the edges reveal the white paper. A green marker is used gently on the back of each leaf so that color bleeds through and absorbs the white edge.

6

The leaves are curled with a small metal knitting needle. With the leaf in the left hand, each section is curled by inserting every segment between the thumb and the side of the needle. The part is pulled through as the needle is rolled on the back of the paper.

7

A precise blueprint drawing for the flutes of the column is drawn on grid paper. It is then attached with masking tape to heavily textured watercolor paper. The furrows are cut with a triangle.

8

The fluted column surface is created with two layers of paper. The bottom layer of paper is curled in a cylindrical shape and glued in place with supports. The slotted paper is then attached to the surface of the cylinder.

9

Once the basic structure of the column is assembled, it is ready for the painting technique. A toothbrush is dipped in the mixed liquid acrylics and spattered lightly across the surface. Gradual layers of paint are applied to create the textured surface.

SALLY VITSKY

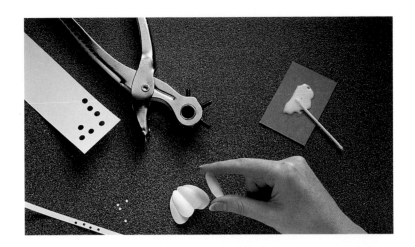

10

The decorative capital on the column is created from 2 ply Bristol paper. Three scalloped symmetrical layers are cut to form the shell. Each piece is curled by gently gliding the paper across the side of a knitting needle. White dots are punched-out using a variable hole punch.

11

The shell is assembled by positioning the curled second layer in the center of the bottom piece. The top curled portion is placed in the middle of the second layer and glued into position.

12

After the column is painted and completely dry, it is ready to be assembled. The shell is glued into place with white Sobo glue. Small white leaves are attached in the upper corners and the tiny white punched dots complete the design.

13

The beach background is cut from a square piece of Canson paper. Several colors of liquid acrylic paints are prepared. A toothbrush is lightly dipped in one color at a time and spattered across the surface. Several layers of paint are applied to create the overall textural surface.

14

After the paint has dried on the Canson paper, it is glued with rubber cement to a piece of foamcore board and trimmed. A band of orange PANTONE® paper is attached on top. This will be used as a thin horizon line for the background.

15

A larger portion of foamcore board is cut for the background. A piece of 2 ply Bristol is airbrushed with a graduated tone of blue for the sky. It is attached with rubber cement and positioned on the foamcore.

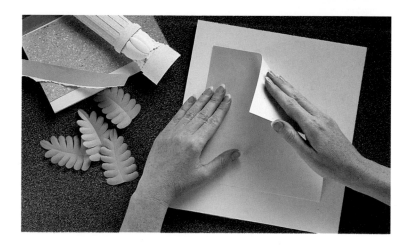

16

The paint spattered beach paper with the orange band is adhered on top of the blue airbrushed background. A PANTONE® blue strip is torn by hand and glued on top of the beach leaving a very thin band of the orange paper exposed.

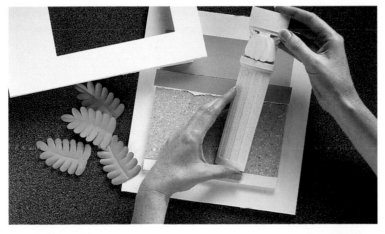

17

The completed column is placed into position on the entire background. Foamcore supports are used to raise it off the back surface for added depth and dimension.

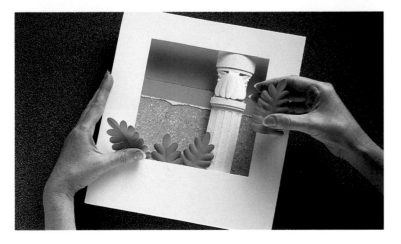

18

The foamcore frame is placed over the entire scene and supported with foamcore legs to create a shadow box effect. The leaves are tucked behind the frame in the foreground.

1

1
Armstrong Tiles *Point Of Purchase and Print Ad*
2
Snack World Magazine *Cover*
3
AAA *Road Atlas Cover*

2

3

SALLY VITSKY

4

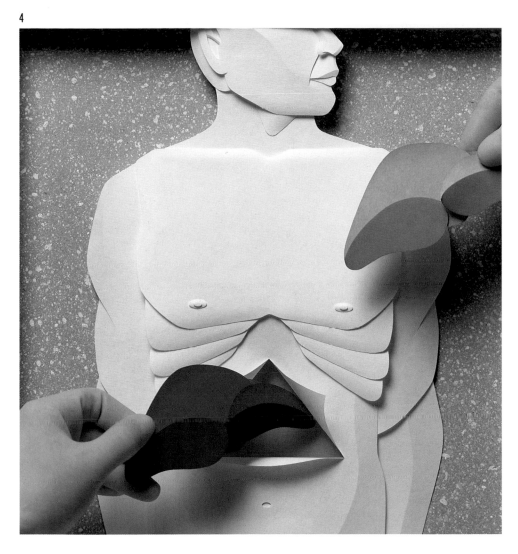

5

6

4
Physicians Weekly *Poster/Liver Transplants*
5
Builder Magazine *Full Page Illustration*
6
Berkley Publishing *Mystery Book Cover "The Gift Horse"*

7

8

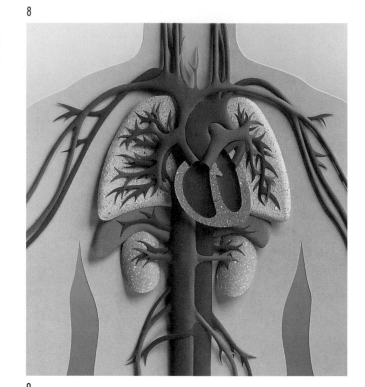

9

7
Physicians Weekly *Poster*
8
Burroughs Wellcome Company *Direct Mail Ad*
9
Reader's Digest *Spot Illustration*

SALLY VITSKY

10

11

12

10
Savers Spices *Point of Purchase Display*
11
Atlantic Monthly *Advertising Insert*
12
Berkley Publishing *Mystery Book Cover "A Grave Without Flowers"*

13

14

15

13
Money Magazine *Inside Illustration*
14
Walden Books *Children's Biography Cover*
15
Walden Books *Children's Biography Cover*

16

17

18

16
Schein Dental Supplies *Magazine Advertisement*
17
Meetings and Conventions Magazine *Inside Illustration*
18
Zero Graphics *Video Cover*

SPECIALTY PAPERS

Specialty papers present the artist with a virtual potpourri from which to express their creative genius. Recycled, handmade, oriental and translucent papers all contribute to the creation of paper sculptures in this unique genre. The sculptures are as distinct as the papers chosen to create them. Specialty paper artists amply demonstrate the true versatility of paper as a sculptural agent. The ingenious application of specialty paper is foremost in the works of Eugene Hoffman and Joan Kritchman-Knuteson.

Eugene Hoffman brings a unique slant to paper sculpture artistry. His ability to pre-visualize in the third dimension captures our interest and jolts our imagination. Hoffman's work with found paper objects transforms his sculptures into compositions in space and time. Joan Kritchman-Knuteson uses handmade, oriental and translucent papers to create her celebrated paper sculptures. She layers tissue thin papers to create depth, shadow and volume. Joan's design sensitivity and attention to detail give her paper sculptures a feeling of warmth and harmony. While these artists work at opposite ends of the paper spectrum, each calls upon a deep reservoir of dynamic creativity.

Joan Kritchman-Knuteson

Joan Kritchman-Knuteson is a self-taught paper sculptor who, for the past 19 years, has worked at the Advertising Art Studio in Milwaukee, Wisconsin. Formally trained in commercial art, she attributes her unique paper sculpture acumen to observation, experimentation, intuition and hard work. Joan's interest in 3-Dimensional art blends well with her regard for nature. The increased availability of specialty papers serves as an additional source of inspiration. Sculpture in general appeals to her mechanical talents. She finds paper an easy and infinitely varied medium of expression.

Joan selects materials with permanence in mind. The rag print, Japanese and handmade papers she favors have either a neutral Ph rating or acid-free content which slows the aging process. For her fine art sculptures, Joan prefers the rag mixed papers since they are less brittle. Joan believes that paper sculpture provides the opportunity to experiment with subtle texture, color and shadow changes. She feels that the tactile appeal of paper sculpture carries a fascination for the artist, but more importantly, for the viewer.

1

Photo copies of initial pencil sketches are made to the exact working size. Color markers are used to delineate color schemes. Additional copies are made for cutting the patterns.

2

Small swatches of paper are laid together for design combinations. Final color is decided while cutting. A variety of oriental, print, handmade and watercolor papers of different weight and texture are selected.

3

Photocopies of the pencil drawings are adhered to the paper with a mixture of 1/4 part rubber cement, 1/2 part rubber cement solvent and 1/4 part One Coat cement. The paper is cut with a #11 blade.

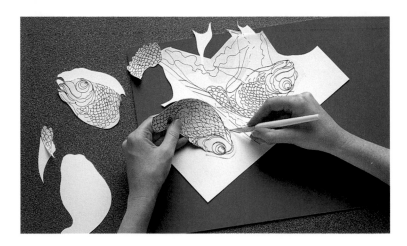

JOAN KRITCHMAN-KNUTESON

4

The foundation for the fish starts out as flat cutouts for the base. After cutting through the two layers of paper, the pattern is removed. The rubber cement mixture allows for easy removal of the delicate rice paper from the original copy.

5

The fins, scales and gills are cut from many thin translucent layers of the oriental and handmade papers. Depending on the number of layers, the elements are curved before or after they are glued together.

6

As the layered sections of the fish are completed, the components are glued together with Duco cement. This quick drying adhesive facilitates the assembly process.

7

The lily petals require specific shaping to achieve the accurate curvature. A dart is created by slicing the petal halfway and overlapping the edges.

8

Numerous petals of alternating size and shape are created then glued individually for the construction of the lily blossom. Additional curling is implemented with the fingernail once the petals are arranged.

9

The lily pad leaves are fabricated from two different layers of paper. The stiff white base is cut slightly larger than the top layer. This acts as a support for the upper portion of the leaf pad fashioned from a delicate handmade paper.

10

A white 1/4" foamcore board is cut for the background. The lily stems are cut from a strong but flexible white paper. The ends of the stems remain attached to the sheet. Then, a sheet of translucent rice paper is slipped under to cover the slots left by the stems.

11

The lily pads and blossoms are placed into position with layers of angled foamcore creating an elevated base. This adds depth and flexibility for the height of the components.

12

The assembled goldfish are positioned with foamcore bases as well. A decorative border is added from strips of handmade papers. Adjustments are made to the overall image as needed.

1
Gallery Artwork *Asparagus Bunch*
2
Commission *Pediatric Neurosurgeon's Office*
3
Gallery Artwork *Scarlet Macaw*

JOAN KRITCHMAN-KNUTESON

4
Gallery Artwork *Unicorn Carrousel*
5
Commission Charles Palmer *Frog Carrousel*
6
Gallery Artwork *Screech Owl*

7
Gallery Artwork *Orchids*
8
Commission Daniel Shays *Wedding Triptych*
9
Gallery Artwork *Zebra Carrousel*

7

9

8

JOAN KRITCHMAN-KNUTESON

10

11

12

10
Gallery Artwork *White Peacocks*
11
Gallery Artwork *Apple Slices*
12
Gallery Artwork *Strawberry Basket*

13

13
Amersham *Advertisement and Catalogue Cover*
14
Gallery Artwork *Swan Seat Carrousel Horse*
15
Gallery Artwork *Bonsai Tree*

14

15

JOAN KRITCHMAN-KNUTESON

16

18

17

16
Jensen Health *Logo Office Display*
17
Gallery Artwork *Day Lily*
18
Hoard's Dairyman *Poster, Brochure and Direct Mailers*

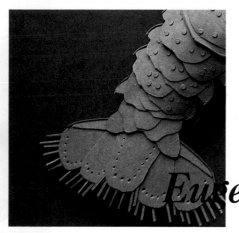

Eugene Hoffman

Eugene Hoffman has been creating 3-Dimensional illustrations for more than 30 years. Presently, he divides his time teaching at the University of Northern Colorado and his studio in Greeley, Colorado. His natural style of sculpting with recycled materials has influenced his work since childhood. As an artist and paper sculptor, he creates all of his assemblages, collages and paper objects from reusable materials. In fabricating his paper sculptures, he uses old scrap cardboard, cereal boxes, paper towels, toilet paper and mailing tubes. His freehand cutting approach of the initial rough sketch, affords him greater freedom and latitude while creating his natural paper sculptures. The range of textures, weights and tonal variations of recycled paper offer infinite possibilities for his work.

The ingenious application of these fragments of daily life places him in a distinct category. He finds this "medium" a limitless palette from which to create. Hoffman turns a random pile of discarded rubbish into a balanced artistic composition. His technique is highly intuitive and calls on his ability to conceptualize his sculptures from pre-existing forms and shapes.

1

Rough sketches are drawn indicating the basic outline structure of the rock lobster (Palinuridae). Each part is numbered on the sketch for easy assembly. The layouts are used as a visual guide when cutting the components.

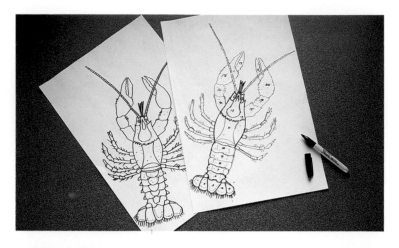

2

Only recycled materials are chosen for the fabrication of the lobster. Scrap cardboard, toilet paper rolls, paper towels and mailing tubes are selected for the construction. The curved structure of the tubes will facilitate curling the cardboard.

3

A medium size mailing tube is chosen for the thorax. The section is cut with scissors straight from the raw cardboard tube without a traced pattern. This method of freehand cutting affords more creative freedom from the layout.

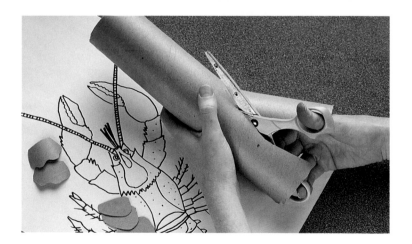

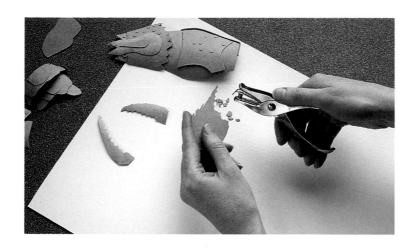

4

The large pincer claw is cut freehand with scissors from a curved section of the cardboard toilet paper roll. A hole punch is used to create a serrated edge along the inner claw areas.

5

Smaller cardboard dots are punched using a variable hole punch. These are glued to the exterior surface of the claws, thorax and tail. With the tip of the knife blade, the small dots are glued using Bordens black label school glue.

6

The segmented legs of the lobster are created from narrow sections of cardboard. The strips are created from scoring several fine horizontal lines along the lateral surface. Care is taken not to cut the cardboard completely through.

7

The narrow scored bands are cut in 1/2" widths. The scored strips are then precisely positioned on top, parallel to the metal edge of the ruler. With both thumbs and forefingers, the pieces are gently folded down causing the cardboard to curve.

8

The curved pieces are cut in short lengths. Slivers of cardboard are sliced accurately along the metal edge of the ruler. These are trimmed in small sections and glued together with the curved lengths to form the setae (bristles) on the spiny legs and tail.

9

The antennae are formed from small shingled flat cardboard elements. They are glued in an overlapping band and held in position by wooden spring clothespins. After the glue has dried, thin strips are cut with a very sharp #11 knife blade along a metal ruler.

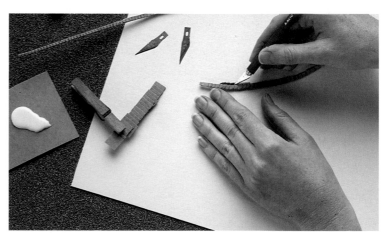

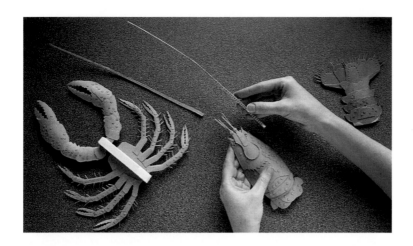

10

The large claws are fastened to a shim support made from layers of foamcore. The spiny legs are attached to a cardboard cutout and are affixed to the underside of the foam strip. The antennae are positioned on the head.

11

The head and thorax assemblage is overlapped onto the antenna and glued. This entire component is attached to the legs and claw assemblage with Bordens black label school glue.

12

The tail section is comprised of many segmented elements and attached with glue. The rear part of the thorax body is overlapped underneath the tail and glued into position. Final adjustments are made on the curvature of the tail and fins.

1

2

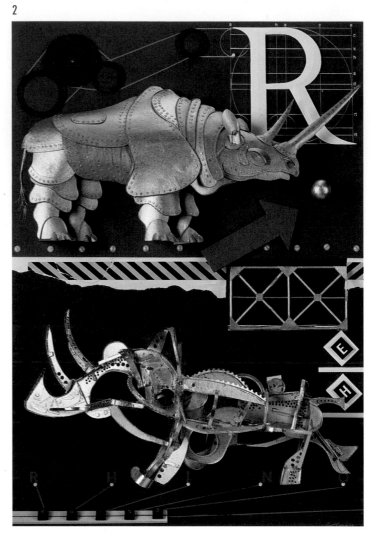

1
Poudre Magazine *Cover*
2
Self Promotion *Rhinoceros*

3

5

4

3
Self Promotion
4
Colorado Film Festival Project
5
Poudre Magazine *Cover*

6
University of N. Colorado *Gala Poster and Direct Mail Insert*
7
Choice Printing *Magazine Insert*
8
The Pressworks Denver *Poster*

6

7

8

EUGENE HOFFMAN

9

11

10

9
The Pressworks Denver *Poster*
10
John Sorbie *Personal Commission*
11
University of N. Colorado *Magazine Cover*

12

13

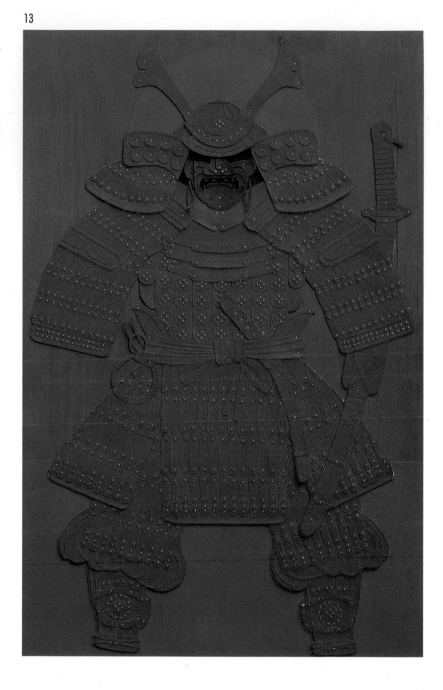

12
Murray Tinkelman's Special Olympics *Baseball Card*
13
Gallery Artwork *Samurai*

EUGENE HOFFMAN

14

15

16

14
The Pressworks Denver *Poster*
15
Flea Illustration
16
University of N. Colorado *Poster and Program Cover/Performing Arts*

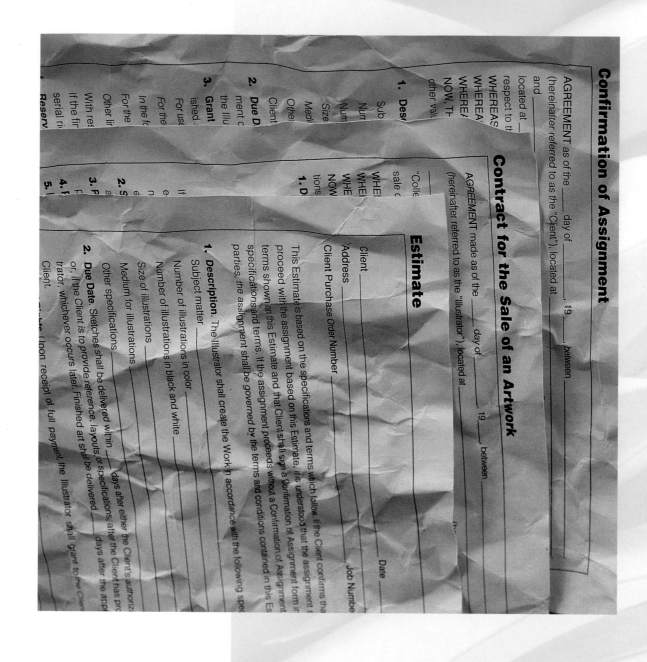

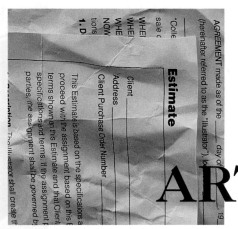

ARTIST'S RIGHTS

The modern paper sculptor has two distinct viable markets to consider. The first is the printed form of photographed paper sculpture in the advertising and publishing industries. The second is the burgeoning field of commissioned paper sculpture models for purchase by individuals and galleries. Each market can provide a lucrative source of income for the serious paper sculpture professional. Photographed paper sculptures used in advertisements are often sold as original works of art. Understanding the artists rights of sale is an important ingredient for successful marketing and copyright protection.

For paper sculptures used in print, fees vary according to magazine use, advertisement size and distribution. First time rights would permit the buyer to use the transparency one time, as per the negotiated fee. Additional fees are paid for each copyright usage thereafter. A contract between the creator of the work and the purchasor should determine the specific rights being transferred. These rights and the value of such rights should be included in the contract. All rights not transferred in the agreement remain the exclusive rights of the artist

In addition, before photographing a work for print use, an agreement must be signed between the photographer and the paper sculptor. This contract should outline the shared rights of ownership between the parties. The usage and fees must be agreed upon before the sale of the sculpture. Contracts pertaining to commissioned paper sculpture models should specify the exact usage being transferred to the client. The artist must determine the specific usage and rights being transferred to the buyer and their fair market value.

Although contracts can offer an artist certain protection under the law, some agreements should be avoided whenever possible. As a freelance artist, you should not sign a work-for-hire contract. Under the work-for-hire provisions of the copyright law, the commissioned artist forfeits all copyright ownership. These rights may include reproduction, distribution and display of the work. Also, the work can be re-used or altered by the buyer without compensation to the artist.

The copyright laws were established to protect the rights of the artist under the Constitution. Any infringement of theses rights can be penalized under the copyright laws. For further information regarding protection of artist's rights, contact the New York based Graphic Artists guild. The Guild was established in 1967 by professional artists concerned with industry guidelines, professional practices, ethics and fair market value for commissioned work. This organization is dedicated to fostering ethical standards between graphic artists and art buyers.

The 3-Dimensional paper sculptor faces unique challenges producing, photographing and marketing their work. The techniques outlined in each chapter will assist you in understanding the myriad applications of paper as an illustrative medium. Paper Sculpture: A Step-By-Step Guide is designed to help you understand the distinct techniques and creative processes presented by the foremost paper sculptors worldwide.

This directory of schools offer paper sculpture as part of their curriculum. These courses detail specific teaching techniques from basic fundamentals to advanced 3-Dimensional paper sculpture methods. They will provide the reader with further advancement as a professional paper sculptor.

ACA COLLEGE OF DESIGN

2528 Kemper Lane
Cincinnati, OH 45206
513.751.1206 Telephone
513.751.1209 Fax

Instructor

Marion Allman

Course Title

Media

Course Description

Involves the teaching techniques used in paper sculpture. Students are required to complete a project using the methods and techniques prescribed.

Course Title

Pop-Ups

Course Description

Students design and develop mechanics for a spread, mailer or children's books.

COLLEGE OF TECHNICAL CAREERS

Commercial Graphics/Design Department
Southern Illinois University
Carbondale, IL 62901-6721
618.453.8863 Telephone

Instructor

David J. White *Assistant Professor*

Course Title

0G315-Advanced Dimensional Design & Illustration for
Commercial Graphics/Design

Course Description

Provides the opportunity to advance skills, development and knowledge in the field of dimensional graphics. Students utilize dimensional design in the conceptualization and production of 1) Advanced dimensional design; Package Design, Point-of-Purchase Displays, etc. 2) Paper engineering for graphic design; "Pop-Up" Ads and Inserts, etc. 3) Paper Sculpture for Dimensional Illustration.

HUSSIAN SCHOOL OF ART, INC.

Commercial Art Department
1010 Arch Street
Philadelphia, PA 19107
215.238.9000 Telephone

Course Title

Experimental Workshop

Course Description

A course to develop experimentation in design and creative thinking for various Commercial Art vehicles such as: Packaging, Point-Of-Purchase display, menus and table tents for promotional projects. Using 3-Dimensional design, paper sculpture and die cuts, as well as working with line, water color, collage, colored pencil and markers. Students learn how to develop, control and execute their design projects.

ROCHESTER INSTITUTE OF TECHNOLOGY

College of Imaging Arts & Sciences

P.O. Box 9887

Rochester, NY 14623-0887

716.475.2646 Telephone

Instructor

Bill Finewood

Course Title

Dimensional Illustration

Course Description

The student examines dimensional visualization, planning through a step-by-step approach, preparation, selection of medium and craftsmanship as vital aspects leading to the production of a three dimensional illustration. The student is exposed to the work of leading dimensional illustrators working in the field today to gain an understanding of the high level of professionalism and dimensional problem solving techniques they employ. Finally, the student examines the relationship of photography as the means of reproducing dimensional illustration in a printed form.

UNIVERSITY OF OREGON

Fine and Applied Arts Department

School of Architecture and Allied Arts

Eugene, OR 97403-1206

503.346.3610 Telephone

Instructor

Miriam Kley

Course Title

Three Dimensional Graphic Design

Course Description

Exploration of various techniques and materials of graphic 3-D illustration such as paper, brass, found objects, wire and paper engineering.

THIS DIRECTORY is designed to give art directors, creative directors and art buyers easy access to the professional paper sculptors represented in this book. The nine artists featured represent Canada, Denmark and the United States. They are recipients of Gold or Silver awards in the Dimensional Illustration Awards Show. Their clients are the benchmark of their professional success as paper sculptors.

GUS ALAVEZOS

19050 Merrymen Circle
Monument, CO 80132
719.531.2266 Telephone (W)
719.488.9078 Telephone (H)

Clients Include:

Atlantic Monthly
AT&T
Canon
Crown Zellerbach
Icelantic Brand
Intel
Kraft
Macmillian/McGraw Publishing
Milton Bradley
Random House
Reader's Digest
Scholastic Books
The Sagamore
Walt Disney Company

Awards

Silver Award Dimensional Illustration Awards Show
Bronze & Merit Awards Dimensional Illustration Awards Show
Society of Illustrators/Los Angeles
Alfie Award

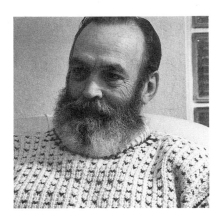

JOHNNA BANDLE
JB Illustration
7726 Noland Road
Lenexa, KS 66216
913.962.9595 Telephone/Fax

Clients Include:
3M
Bell South
Delta Airlines
Georgia Pacific
Hallmark Cards, Inc.
IBM
J.C.Penney
John Deere & Company
Kae Jewelers
Kimberly Clark
McDonalds
NEC/Japan/England/United States
Sprint
Visa
Zales Jewelers

Awards
Gold & Silver Awards Dimensional Illustration Awards Show
Bronze & Merit Awards Dimensional Illustration Awards Show
Best Use of Paper Award (Butler Paper)

EUGENE HOFFMAN
1811 12th Street
Greeley, CO 80631
303.351.7991 Telephone

Clients Include:
City of Greeley
Communications Arts
Denver Museum of Natural History
Graphis
Houghton Mifflin Publishing
Idea Magazine/Tokyo
Print Magazine
University of Northern Colorado
Wells Fargo

Awards
Gold & Silver Awards Dimensional Illustration Awards Show
Bronze & Merit Awards Dimensional Illustration Awards Show
Gold & Silver Metals Society of Illustrators New York
Gold Metals Denver Art Directors Club
Dallas/Ft. Worth 100 Best Art Directors Club
Merit Awards Los Angeles Art Directors Club

JOAN KRITCHMAN-KNUTESON
Advertising Arts Studio, Inc.
710 N. Plankinton Avenue/#800
Milwaukee, WI 53203-2454
414.276.6306 Telephone
414.276.7925 Fax

Clients Include:
Allan Bradley Company
Amersham
Appleton Paper Company
Chris Craft
Dow Chemical
Hoard's Dairyman
Kohler Company
Medical Economics Publishing
Mustad Fishhook Company
Racine Wisconsin Zoo
Solvay Animal Health, Inc.
Upjohn
Wayne Feeds Company

Awards
Gold & Silver Awards Dimensional Illustration Awards Show
Bronze & Merit Awards Dimensional Illustration Awards Show
NOMA National Agramarketing Association
BBPA Bell Awards

HAL LOSE
Toad Hall Graphics
533 W. Hortter Street/Toad Hall
Philadelphia, PA 19119
215.849.7635 Telephone/Fax

Clients Include:
AT&T
Bell Atlantic
Bally's Hotel & Casino
Ciba Geigy Pharmaceuticals
Hampton Brown Publishing
Macmillian/McGraw Hill Publishing
MGM Grand/Las Vegas
New York Real Estate Digest
Nursing Magazine
Rohm & Haas
Schenley's Liquors
Scott Paper Company
Smith Kline Beecham International
Whittle Communications: Channel 1
World Book Medical Encyclopedia

Awards
Silver Award Dimensional Illustration Awards Show
Bronze & Merit Awards Dimensional Illustration Awards Show
Merit Award Society of Illustrators Humor 2 Show

JONATHAN MILNE

Papersculptureworks, Inc.

15556 58A Avenue

Surrey, B.C. V3S 8E7 Canada

604.576.0582 Telephone/Fax

Clients Include:

American Express

Banca Fideuram/Rome

BBC TV Titles/UK

IBM

Kodak

Licher Bier/Germany

Macmillian/McGraw Hill Publishing

New York Times

Time Life

Zeneca ICI/UK

Awards

Gold & Silver Awards Dimensional Illustration Awards Show

Bronze & Merit Awards Dimensional Illustration Awards Show

New York Art Directors Club Show

Art Directors Club of Melbourne

Art Directors Club/Toronto

Graphis

LEO MONAHAN

Leo Monahan & Associates, Inc.

1912 Hilton Drive

Burbank, CA 91504

818.843.6115 Telephone

818.841.5886 Fax

Clients Include:

AT&T

Esquire

Children's Television

China Airlines

Coke Cola

Eddie Bauer

General Motors

Godiva Chocolates

Hewlett Packard

IBM International Papers

Joffrey Ballet

NBC

Time Life

Awards

Gold & Silver Awards Dimensional Illustration Awards Show

Bronze & Merit Awards Dimensional Illustration Awards Show

Life Achievement Award Society of Illustrators/Los Angeles

SØREN THAAE
3-D Illustrations
38, Auroravej
Rodovre, Copenhagen DK-2610
Denmark
45.31.41.14.11 Telephone/Fax

Clients Include:
Baltica Insurance Company
Duracell
Elnyt
Royal Copenhagen
Shell/Denmark
Superfos Korn

Awards
Gold Award Dimensional Illustration Awards Show
Bronze & Merit Awards Dimensional Illustration Awards Show

SALLY VITSKY
Sally Vitsky Illustration
4116 Bromley Lane
Richmond, VA 23221
804.359.4726 Telephone/Fax

Clients Include:
AAA
Business Week
General Electric
Greyhound Bus
Harcourt Brace Jovanovich, Inc.
IBM
Institutional Investor
Macmillian/McGraw Hill Publishing
Monsanto
Newsweek
NY NEX
Reader's Digest

Awards
Silver Award Dimensional Illustration Awards Show
Bronze & Merit Awards Dimensional Illustration Awards Show
D.C. Illustrators Club Annual Show

DIMENSIONAL ILLUSTRATORS, INC. was established by Kathleen Ziegler and Nick Greco to create and promote excellence in 3-Dimensional illustration. Kathleen is President and Creative Director of this award winning 3-D design studio. The studio specializes in creating models and props for the pharmaceutical, advertising, publishing and TV industries. Kathleen's design mediums include plastic, clay, wood, acrylics, paper and foam. She has garnered awards for technical excellence and innovative 3-D designs from the Association of Medical Illustrators, the Desi Awards Show, the Philadelphia Art Directors Club Show and the AGFA Achievement in Design Award.

An accomplished lecturer, Kathleen has participated in numerous seminars on 3-Dimensional illustration including the Association of Medical Illustrators, The University of the Arts in Philadelphia, Graphix '90 in New York and the Royal College of Art in London, England. She has been featured in Step-By-Step Graphics and her work has appeared on the covers of the industry's leading magazines.

Nick Greco is Vice President and principal partner of Dimensional Illustrators, Inc. He concentrates on the marketing aspects of the 3-Dimensional design industry. Nick negotiates contracts, evaluates projects and establishes sale and buyout rights. He has lectured in the United States and abroad on copyright laws, resale rights and contracts for 3-Dimensional illustrators. Dimensional Illustrators, Inc. is proud of its role in promoting the recognition of 3-D illustrators, art directors and modelmakers worldwide.

THE DIMENSIONAL ILLUSTRATION AWARDS SHOW was established by Dimensional Illustrators, Inc. as an international competition to acknowledge excellence in 3-Dimensional illustration. This singular show honors 3-Dimensional illustrators, art directors and modelmakers in a competition that affords them the exposure and plaudits worthy of this hybrid medium. Entries are accepted in the following categories: magazine advertisements and editorials, brochures, annual reports, TV commercials, calendars, greeting cards and self-promotions. Mediums include: paper, plastic, wood and clay sculpture, paper and fabric collage, paper pop-ups, mixed media, recycled materials and video animation as applied to the communications industry.

The Dimensional Illustration Awards Show is exhibited bi-annually at the Art Directors Club of New York and the Fouts & Fowler Gallery in London, England. This international show has presented Gold, Silver and Bronze awards to 3-D illustrators and art directors from Asia, Australia, Canada, Europe, South America and the United States. Entries may be submitted annually from April 1st thru May 31st. If you wish information concerning the awards show or the 3-D illustration awards annual, please contact:

Nick Greco
Dimensional Illustrators, Inc.
362 Second Street Pike/Suite 112
Southampton, PA 18966 USA
215.953.1415 Telephone 215.953.1697 Fax

DEBORAH DAVIS is a graphic designer and typographer who lives and works in the Los Angeles area. Her design experience ranges from book and type design to print production. Deborah has worked as a freelance graphic designer in all phases of book publishing. She enjoys designing books, book covers, posters and various materials for the advertising and publishing industry. As a designer, she is familiar with all aspects of the graphic design profession including pre-press, print and production.

JENNIFER DUNN is a freelance designer who lives in Philadelphia with her husband and two prized cats. She holds a Masters Degree in Visual Design from Southeastern Massachusetts University. Jennifer concentrates her graphic efforts on book designs and has worked as a consultant with many of the areas leading publishers. In addition, she applies her talents to the creation of brochures, promotional materials and posters. Her style, awareness and attention to detail contribute to her overall design sensitivity.

TOM MC CLINTOCK has worked as a freelance journalist since 1972. Presently, he works in the Philadelphia area and holds a Bachelor of Arts Degree in English Literature and Creative Writing. Tom specializes in personal interviews, music and entertainment columns and general feature writing. He currently applies his writing talents to articles on fiction, travel and leisure. As a freelance writer, he enjoys the freedom to explore a wide range of topics relating to the arts and entertainment industry.

KEN YANOVIAK is a Philadelphia based freelance photographer who specializes in magazine editorials and public relations work. His clients include Philadelphia Magazine, Clean Water Action and Bryn Mawr Hospital. Ken has had numerous photographic exhibitions in the United States and abroad. His work was recently featured in the Photo Synkyria '92 exhibition in Greece. Through his photographs, he captures the human elements of the many cultures he has visited.

Graphic Artists Guild. ***Graphic Artists Guild Handbook Pricing & Ethical Guidelines.*** 6th ed. Graphic Artists Guild, 1982

Ritchie, Carson, I.A. ***Art in Paper. U.S.A.*** A.S. Barnes & Company, South Brunswick and N.Y. Thomas Yoseloff Ltd., London. A.S. Barnes Co., Inc., Cranbury N.J., 1976

Sadler, Arthur. ***Paper Sculpture***. 5th revised ed. New York, Toronto, London: Pitman Publishing Corporation.

This book was set in Caslon 3, Futura Book and Futura Condensed manufactured by Adobe. It was designed and produced on the Macintosh using Aldus PageMaker 4.2. Final output was on a Linotronic 330.